D0131163

White, Michael, 1959–
Galileo Galilei :
Inventor, astronomer and
1999.
33305208217301
sa   04/18/05

OF SCIENCE

Galileo Galilei

Inventor,
Astronomer,
and Rebel

Michael White

BLACK   , INC.

WOODB   CTICUT

SANTA CLARA COUNTY LIBRARY

3 3305 20821 7301

Published by Blackbirch Press, Inc.
260 Amity Road
Woodbridge, CT 06525
web site: http://www.blackbirch.com
e-mail: staff@blackbirch.com

© 1999 Blackbirch Press, Inc.
First U.S. Edition

All rights reserved. No part of this book may be reproduced in any form without permission
in writing from Blackbirch Press, Inc., except by a reviewer.

First published in Great Britain as *Scientists Who Have Changed the World* by Exley Publications
Ltd., Chalk Hill, Watford, 1991.
© Exley Publications, Ltd.
© Michael White

10 9 8 7 6 5 4 3 2

Photo Credits
Alinari: 36/37; The Bridgeman Art Library: 4; Mary Evans Picture Library: 6, 7, 9, 10 and 42
(Explorer); Robert Harding Picture Library: 26 (W. Rawlings); Michael Holford: 18, 19 all, 28;
Hulton Picture Library: 15; The Image Bank: 5 (W. Bibikow), 27 (P. DeRenzis), 30/31, 58 (C.
Place); the Mansell Collection: 20, 43, 56; Photographie Buloz: 54/5; Ann Ronan Picture
Library: 8 top, 22, 25, 38 and 39 top and bottom (Goldschmidt & Co.), 49 top (Royal
Astronomical Society), 60 (Goldschmidt & Co.); Scala: cover 8 bottom, 12, 13, 16, 33, 44,
48, 51, 59; Science Photo Library: 35 (Dr. H Edgerton), 41 (NOAO), 45 top and bottom
(NASA), 49 bottom (Dr. J. Burgess): Weidenfeld & Nicolson Archives: 11, 46, 50, 52/53.

Printed in China

Library of Congress Cataloging-in-Publication Data
White, Michael, 1959–.
    Galileo Galilei: inventor, astronomer, and rebel / by Michael White.
        p. cm.—(Giants of science)
    Includes bibliographical references and index.
    Summary: Describes the life and work of the scientist who was persecuted by the
Inquisition for his views of the universe.
    ISBN 1-56711-325-7
    1. Galilei, Galileo, 1564–1642—Juvenile literature. 2. Astronomy—History—Juvenile
literature. 3. Galilei, Galileo, 1564–1642—Trials, litigation, etc.—Juvenile literature.
4. Inquisition—Juvenile literature. 5. Astronomers—Italy—Biography—Juvenile literature.
[1. Galilei, Galileo, 1564–1642. 2. Scientists.] I. Title. II. Series.
QB36.G2W48 1999   98–49141
520.92—dc21   CIP
[b]   AC

Contents

On Trial

The courtroom in Vatican City in Rome is full. Crammed into the tiers forming a semicircle around the walls are cardinals, bishops, theologians, and philosophers. Presiding over the whole affair is Pope Urban VIII, leader of the Roman Catholic Church. It is April 1633 and a sixty-nine-year-old man is on trial. He stands in the dock, upright and dignified, despite the humiliations he has been put through. His clothes are well-cut but a little unkempt. His hair is silver, his face is worn and tired.

Despite a severe illness, the old man has been summoned to Rome. He has traveled from Florence, through plague-ridden Italy because he has angered the church leaders by claiming that Earth is not the central point of the universe. The man is Galileo Galilei, the greatest scientist and mathematician of his age.

In the middle of the massive court room sits Pope Urban. He has formed powerful political alliances with other countries to halt the progress of Protestantism. He feels that Galileo's work is damaging to the Catholic Church. For most of the trial, his head is bowed in concentration as he listens to the case against Galileo. But, every once in a while, the pope frowns at the mathematician. Urban is furious and wants Galileo punished. As he sees it, Galileo has committed one of the worst heresies possible and his teachings have seriously threatened the Church's authority.

To the pope's left sits his closest servants, the cardinals who head the dreaded Inquisition, the

Opposite: *Galileo was put on trial in April 1633 at the age of sixty-nine. In this picture, you can see him standing in the dock in the corner of the court (top left).*

Below: *Modern astronomy owes a large debt to the work of Galileo. He was one of the great astronomers who laid the foundation for our modern view of the solar system.*

Church's secret police. These men could have Galileo tortured and executed for what he has said and done. They could personally supervise proceedings as the old man is stretched on the rack, or has burning metal shards thrust under his fingernails. Thirty-three years earlier, in 1600, the Inquisition had ordered the philosopher Giorgano Bruno to be burned at the stake for heresy. These men have tortured and executed countless others in the intervening years.

Guilty

As Galileo faces his most desperate hour, he has one great advantage over any of the other heretics who have faced trial and eventual execution at the hands of the Inquisition. He has gone out of his way to make numerous friends in high places and can count on many of those sitting beside the pope to come to his aid.

Although many of the powerful men of the Inquisition disagree with Galileo's ideas, they understand the complex mind of the great scientist. Deep beneath the public image they have to portray, they are desperate to save his life.

During the agonizing weeks of the trial, as Galileo stands in the dock, the Inquisition interrogates him with many questions. To all outward appearances, they show no mercy for the scientist.

In private, however, Galileo's friends subtly play down his crimes in an effort to calm the situation and persuade the head of the Church to save the scientist's life.

Each day at the trial, Galileo continues to claim his innocence and modify his opinions in an effort to come to some compromise.

On the final day of the trial, Galileo is brought to the dock for the last time. The court falls silent as the pope enters and sits down. The representative of

Nicolaus Copernicus was born in 1473—nearly a century before Galileo, yet his revolutionary views on the nature and movement of the stars and planets greatly influenced the Italian astronomer. Copernicus described some of these ideas in short manuscripts during his lifetime.

the Inquisition strides to the front of the court and opens the document that will reveal Galileo's fate.

Galileo, he pronounces, is guilty and is to be imprisoned for the rest of his life.

"The Dialogue"

The trial of Galileo in 1633 was the climax to the series of events that had begun nearly 100 years earlier. It began with the publication of a book called *The Revolution of the Heavenly Spheres*, written by Polish astronomer Nicolaus Copernicus. In this book, Copernicus claimed that Earth was simply a planet orbiting the sun. This proposal went directly against the accepted Earth-centered universe theories of the time, and was branded as heresy by the Catholic Church.

In the heart of civilized Europe in 1633, Galileo Galilei—the most respected scientist of his generation—was hauled up in front of the Inquisition. He was accused of the terrible crime of heresy simply because he supported the views suggested in Copernicus's book.

Nine years earlier, Galileo had been asked by Pope Urban VIII to write a book that would give a balanced account of the argument over the nature of the universe. What this really meant was that the pope wanted Galileo to discuss the various arguments, but finally agree with the Church, not Copernicus. The result of Galileo's work was a book called *Dialogue Concerning the Two Chief Systems of the World*.

The problem was that Galileo did not do as he was told. The accepted theories of the universe were based on the idea that Earth was the central point of the universe. But, in his book, Galileo completely destroyed this idea and sided with Copernicus. He said that the Sun, not Earth, was the central point.

Throughout his life Galileo managed to remain on the right side of the Church despite his scientific theories, which went against church doctrine.

Above: *The front cover of Galileo's* The Dialogue.

Below: *Pope Urban VIII holding court surrounded by fawning believers.*

When Urban's advisors read a copy of *The Dialogue,* Galileo's conclusion was immediately obvious and he was summoned to Rome. Doctors attending Galileo protested that moving him would endanger his life. The pope declared that if Galileo did not come of his own free will, he would be brought to them in chains.

The Church

Seventeenth-century European study was controlled by two powerful forces—the Roman Catholic Church headed by the pope, and ancient philosophy dominated by the 2,000-year-old ideas of the Greek philosopher, Aristotle. The Church had an overwhelming influence on the lives of most Europeans, and this was especially the case with the devoutly Catholic Italians. During Galileo's childhood, one in twelve people living in Rome was either a cleric or a nun.

The Catholic Church controlled the people by completely forbidding any teaching that deviated from what was taught in the Bible.

To enforce this control, the Church set up the Inquisition. This was a group of Church leaders who were organized to monitor publications and public declarations. They censored books that did not totally agree with the traditional Catholic teaching, and they persecuted and tried anyone who persisted in publishing heretical views.

The Church also set up the Order of the Jesuits, who worked on scientific problems and taught their version of the truth. Jesuit philosophy and science was what Aristotle had taught. Any discovery made by a Jesuit researcher had to fit into the accepted, inherited world-view of Aristotle. If an observation did not fit with Greek teaching, it had to be false. If Aristotle was wrong, by implication so, too, was the Bible.

Aristotle was a born in southern Greece in 384 B.C. He was a great thinker and developed theories of how the universe operated 2,000 years before the birth of modern science. He had many startlingly accurate ideas about basic science, but was also totally wrong about many things.

Among Aristotle's many misconceptions was his belief that the Moon, along with other celestial bodies, was featureless and absolutely perfect in form. Instead of suggesting the idea that physical laws worked in the same way throughout the universe, he believed that there was one set of physical laws that operated on Earth and a different set for the celestial sphere—the name he gave everything outside Earth. He believed that comets were produced inside Earth's atmosphere and had nothing to do with the celestial sphere.

This illustration shows Copernicus's view of the solar system with the Sun at the center. This is called the heliocentric system.

Above all, the biggest error in Aristotle's thinking was his notion of Earth's position in space. He believed that Earth was fixed as the central point of the universe. In Aristotle's philosophy, Earth did not revolve or move in any way; instead, the Sun, the Moon, and all the known planets revolved around Earth.

Because his theories put humans at the center of the universe, Aristotle's model was very popular with the Church. After all, "Man was made in God's image." It was surely correct, therefore, that Earth should take its rightful place as the central point of all creation.

Conflict

This was the state of affairs when, in 1543, Copernicus stated his revolutionary theory that Earth, along with the other planets, revolved around the Sun.

Copernicus was scorned, not because his theory could be proven by experiment to be false, but simply because it went against what had been taught by Aristotle and the Bible.

This is what the intellectual world was like before Galileo was born. It was dominated by philosophers obsessed with Aristotelian ideas who were ignorant of genuine scientific principles, and by theologians who took every word of the Bible literally. If it had not been for the work of Galileo, who challenged this accepted wisdom, scientific advancement could have perhaps been postponed for hundreds of years.

Rebellious Views

Galileo Galilei was born the eldest child to Vincenzio and Giulia Galilei on February 15, 1564. The family lived in the city of Pisa, situated in the Tuscany region of northwest Italy.

Johannes Kepler was a contemporary of Galileo's and a great supporter of Copernicus's Sun-centered theories.

Galileo's father was a well-known musician who was interested in musical theory. He became quite famous in Italy as the originator of a number of revolutionary views of music, and was the first person to use mathematics in its study. Galileo himself learned to play the lute while he was still young, and became quite an accomplished musician. Although he was outgoing and energetic, he enjoyed sitting alone in the courtyard or in his room playing the lute or composing his own songs.

As well as being a celebrated musician, Galileo's father gained a reputation as a rebellious thinker. Vincenzio hated closed-minded people, especially those in positions of authority in the academic world. The young Galileo was influenced by his father's attitude. In his later work, there are echoes of his father's anti-establishment opinions. In many ways, Galileo argued against narrow-mindedness in the world of science in much the same way that his father had raged against narrow-mindedness in music.

The era commonly referred to as the Renaissance began in the Tuscany region where Galileo grew up, about 100 years before his birth. It was an astonishing time of "re-awakening" in the arts and sciences. The improvement in printing methods meant an ever increasing number of books were being published. With this, came a greater ability to communicate ideas and scientific developments.

During the Renaissance, people were eager for information, for reality instead of religious symbols, for new discoveries about the planet they lived on, for art and literature. Before the Renaissance, there had been an unquestioning acceptance of medieval ideas. Now there was a need for challenge and knowledge. This was the atmosphere into which Galileo was born. Not only

Above: *The house near the Porta Fiorentina at Pisa, where Galileo was born on February 15, 1564.*

• •

"It appears to me that they who in proof of anything simply rely on the weight of authority, without adducing any argument in support of it, act very absurdly. I, on the contrary, wish to be allowed to raise questions freely and to answer without any adulation of authorities, as becomes those who are truly in search of the truth."

–Vincenzio Galilei, Galileo's father

• •

Italian glass makers of the Renaissance were some of the country's greatest craftsmen and most highly skilled artists. Ornate glasswork such as this was just one expression of the flourishing arts of the Renaissance.

was he a versatile thinker, he was an open-minded intellectual, always ready to accept new ideas and progressive views. He used the latest techniques available to him to communicate his discoveries to others. He published a collection of revolutionary books, and did more than any of his contemporaries to push science into a new era.

To the Heart of the Renaissance

Until the age of eleven, Galileo was educated at home by his father and a series of private tutors. He was a lively, outgoing child who loved to explore and investigate everything. When he was not in lessons, he would go off on his own to discover tunnels and deserted buildings in the city or wander the lush countryside of tranquil Tuscany.

When it came time for Galileo to get a more formal education, the choices were not easy. His father distrusted most educational establishments and strongly resisted the thought of sending his eldest son to be indoctrinated at one of them.

In 1575, the family moved to Florence, a large city east of Pisa. Of all the Italian cities, Florence is considered to be the place where Renaissance learning and intellectual life was at its greatest. Many historians believe that it was in Florence that the Renaissance began. When Galileo's family moved there, it was at the pinnacle of its development as the intellectual heart of Europe. Vincenzio could not afford to pay for his son's education, so the eleven-year-old Galileo was sent away to a monastery school.

Things, however, did not run as smoothly as his father had hoped. Within three years, Vincenzio felt forced to remove him from the school when he discovered that the studious young man had volunteered himself as a novice monk. Vincenzio was horrified by the idea, and brought Galileo back to Florence to continue his education.

Conflicts

This incident was to be the first of many conflicts between Galileo and his father. Although they shared views on the rigid and limited outlook of the academic world, they disagreed on the best course for Galileo's career.

In 1581, when he was seventeen, Galileo was enrolled at the University of Pisa. His father insisted that he study medicine because many believed it to be the best first step on the ladder of success for an academic in sixteenth-century Italy.

Galileo reluctantly went along with his father's wishes, even though his true talents were in other areas. Among other things, Galileo was a gifted

This painting of Florence by Giorgio Vasari was painted about the time Galileo's family moved to the city in 1575. It shows the large, walled city, with sprawling suburbs beyond the Arno river and the fortifications.

....

"I think that in discussions of physical problems we ought to begin not from the authority of scriptural passages, but from sense-experiences and necessary demonstrations. . . . Nor is God any less excellently revealed in Nature's actions than in the sacred statements of the Bible."

—Galileo

....

musician, an excellent painter, and an extremely good writer.

During his first term at Pisa University, Galileo began attending mathematics lectures in his spare time and became captivated by the stark beauty of the subject. In particular, he was fascinated by lectures delivered by the court mathematician Ostillo Ricci on the subject of Euclidean geometry.

Galileo attended Ricci's lectures week after week. Before long, the court mathematician began to notice the well-built, handsome young man who always sat at the back of the lecture hall, listening intently to every word. At the end of each talk Galileo would ask Ricci innumerable searching questions. The mathematician realized that he had a very talented student at his lectures and encouraged him to study mathematics rather than medicine at the university.

Despite his father's protests, Galileo went ahead and changed courses. By the end of his first term, Galileo was a mathematics undergraduate.

"The Wrangler"

Galileo became impatient with some philosophers' attitudes toward science, and he often participated in heated arguments and private discussions. On many occasions, he would become excited and raise his voice, loudly disputing the views of his colleagues and lecturers.

Galileo undoubtedly had a mischievous streak, but he was a respected and well-disciplined student. He was well liked by the other students and gained a reputation for his quick wit. When it came to questions of mathematics and physics, however, he had no fears about making his views clear. In fact, he argued so much at the university that he got himself the nickname *Il Attaccabrighe*, "The Wrangler."

His main argument was that science could never progress without questioning what the Greeks had done. Aristotle had not conducted a single experiment in his entire life. He reached conclusions simply by a process of applying logic. And that, Galileo argued, was not enough. Aristotle's entire system was interconnected—one principle led to another, and each idea supported the others. If one part of his philosophy was wrong, all of his other conclusions were.

Galileo's approach was the opposite of Aristotle's. At Pisa, he argued that science could only be based on experiment. An idea might be based on inspiration first, but it could only be proven or accepted through experiment—an idea that is taken for granted today.

Most of Galileo's colleagues at the university disagreed with his notions. Knowing the belief of the Church, Galileo was wise enough to argue his views as being merely one of many suggestions, and gave no more weight to his anti-Aristotelian

Between 1581 and 1585, Galileo attended university in his childhood town of Pisa.

thoughts than to any others. That, at least, was his approach in public....

The Pendulum Swing

Galileo made his first important scientific discovery while at the University of Pisa. And, ironically, it was thanks to the Church.

Although in later life Galileo would come into serious conflict with the Church, throughout his life he was a devout Catholic and attended mass at Pisa Cathedral every Sunday.

As fate would have it, on one particular Sunday the service was taken by a visiting priest who delivered a very dull sermon. Before long, Galileo became bored and his eyes began to wander. It was then he spotted, high overhead, a swinging lamp. Suddenly, a thought struck him. He had seen objects swinging many times before, but he had never realized a startling fact about them.

Sometimes, the distance the lamp swung would be shorter, sometimes longer, as it moved by the air currents. However, no matter what the distance was, the lamp always seemed to take the same amount of time to complete one swing.

He had no timepiece or clock to measure the exact time of the swing, so he used his own pulse, as he had done with many experiments at the university.

Before the boring sermon was over, the truth was clear to see—each swing took the same length of time to go from one end of the path to the other. This occurred if the lamp went through a long swing, or a small swing.

After mass, Galileo rushed back to his quarters at the university and began to experiment with a number of homemade copies of the lamp by attaching weights to pieces of string. Again, he timed the swings as carefully as he could with the

Opposite: *One Sunday in 1583 Galileo made his first important scientific discovery, which involved the motion of a pendulum.*

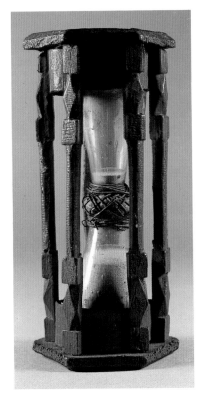

Above: *The sandglass was one of the only ways of measuring time before Galileo's discoveries.*

Opposite, top left: *The basic framework of a pendulum clock, designed by Galileo late in his life.*

Opposite, top right: *One of the world's earliest clocks, built about fifty years after Galileo's death and constructed on the principles he had first developed.*

Opposite, below: *A sundial that tells the time by observing the shadow cast across its face by the sunlight falling on a string.*

only timepiece available—his pulse. Although this method of measuring the passage of time was not totally accurate, it showed quite quickly that his original notion had been correct.

Galileo had discovered the pendulum, and stated the simple law that "whatever the length of the pendulum swing, the time taken to complete the swing is the same." Scientists call this the pendulum's periodic swing.

The First Accurate Clock

After the discovery, Galileo decided to pursue the matter further. He made a huge variety of pendulums using different weights or "bobs," changing the length of the string, changing the shape of the bob, as well as the type of string it was attached to. Noting the results of his experiments, he began to look for patterns in the data. Gradually, a number of simple laws became apparent.

First, he discovered that the period—or length of time—of the swing was not affected at all by the weight of the bob. If the same length of string was used and only the weight of the bob was changed, the periodic time was the same.

Next, by using the same bob but using different lengths of string, Galileo saw that the length of string was a crucial factor. In fact, after repeating the experiment a number of times a very clear relationship began to emerge. The time needed to complete a swing depended only on the square root of the length of the string.

Galileo could not really explain why this rule applied. In fact, it was not until the next century, when more was known about gravity and forces acting on objects, that an explanation was found.

Galileo was quick to realize that his new discovery had a number of applications. His first idea was to use pendulums to construct an accurate clock.

Until the sixteenth century, scientists had serious difficulties measuring short time periods. Galileo himself was becoming increasingly frustrated with the inaccurate machines that were available. In fact, his method of using his own pulse was more accurate than any manufactured timepiece of the day.

Near the end of Galileo's life, the idea of using pendulums in clocks was eventually accepted. The discoverer himself, however, gained nothing from it.

The End of Student Life

In 1585, at age twenty-one, Galileo left the university without obtaining a degree. Although this seems strange today, it was quite common in sixteenth-century Italy, where official qualifications were not as important as one's reputation.

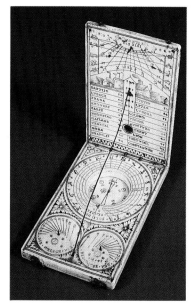

Galileo moved back to the district where his family lived, between Florence and Siena. He immediately set about to find employment and earn a living. His father could no longer support him, and he had only his mathematical skills and university experience to rely on.

Galileo was a very likable young man and had winning charm. This would not be the last time in his life that his open friendliness would be a great asset to him. He went out of his way to make friends with a number of wealthy families in the area and let it be known that he was willing to teach science to their children, or anyone willing to pay for his services.

In his spare time, the young scientist continued his private research in mathematical physics. Very gradually, he began to gain a reputation among Florentine mathematicians and philosophers. He had become well known at the University of Pisa for his unconventional views on scientific wisdom and for his discoveries of the periodic law of the pendulum. He was accepted by his peers as a gifted, but not yet fully proven, mathematician.

The Storyteller

While working as a tutor, Galileo wrote his first full-scale physics text. It was called *Il bilancetta* and, although it was a fairly small book, it contained a number of descriptions of experiments he had been conducting. Of particular interests to other scientists was a set of the author's suggestions on how to improve the ideas of the great Greek philosopher Archimedes.

Archimedes was the greatest Greek scientist. He lived 100 years after Aristotle, and is considered to have been a genius whose mathematical skill was only to be matched by Isaac Newton's, more than 2,000 years later.

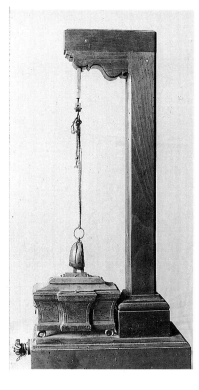

This is the actual pendulum used by Galileo in his experiments, conducted after seeing the lamp's motion in the church.

Archimedes's most famous discovery was the fact that when a solid object is submersed in fluid—for example gas or liquid—the weight of the fluid displaced is equal to the apparent loss of weight of the object.

According to the legend, Archimedes discovered this scientific breakthrough because of a cheating goldsmith. Archimedes's patron, King Heiron, had commissioned a new gold crown, but had suspected it was not made of pure gold. He asked his friend Archimedes to prove the matter one way or the other.

Archimedes realized that if the crown was not made of pure gold, its metal would have a different density than pure gold. The density of an object shows how much material is packed into a certain space. The more material there is in a certain space, the more dense it is. Lead, for instance, is very dense because there is a large number of atoms packed into a small space.

Density is equal to the mass of an object divided by its volume. If an object occupies a small space but has a large mass—meaning it is heavy—it is said to be dense. If an object occupies a large space and has a small mass it is not very dense.

Archimedes realized that, in order to calculate the density of the crown, he would have to know both its mass and the space it took up—its volume. Finding the mass of the crown would be easy, but the only way to work out its volume would be to pound it into a cube or a sphere. King Heiron was quite understandably against this method.

It was then that Archimedes found a solution. He would submerge the crown in water and then do the same with an equal mass of pure gold. The amount of water displaced each time could then be calculated. If the same amount of water was displaced, then the density of the metal in the crown would have to be equal to the density of pure gold and the crown would be genuine. If the amounts were different, the crown could not be made of pure gold.

Much to the goldsmith's misfortune, the amounts of displaced water were not equal, and Archimedes was able to say for sure that the King had in fact been tricked!

Galileo recounted the story in great length in *Il bilancetta* before adding his own refinements. From that first widely published work, Galileo would always describe his discoveries in the form of a story. Sometimes the ideas would be explained in dialogue of a play, or he would tell a story and put across his ideas as part of the plot. Galileo would often use the biting comedy called satire.

Satire relies on making fun of serious matters in a very subtle way. By using comedy, Galileo

Legend has it that Archimedes realized his ideas about density and the displacement of water when he saw the water level in his bath rising as he got into it.

became very popular among well-educated, inquisitive readers. But, his methods also helped fuel the arguments against him. On a number of occasions his critics said that he had gone too far, and that his satire was more like heresy.

The satire technique ultimately proved very successful, and despite their fairly innovative nature, Galileo's suggestions in *Il bilancetta* were accepted by most other scientists. This was because his ideas were only adding to accepted views, pushing understanding forward just a little, rather than proposing a radical new approach at odds with Aristotle, Archimedes, or any other Greek philosopher.

Influential Friends

Around this time, Galileo met the Marquis Guidobaldo del Monte, who was to have a significant influence on the scientist's fortunes. Del Monte was a wealthy amateur engineer and patron of science and philosophy.

He was impressed with Galileo's work on the pendulum and his successful *Il bilancetta*. He tried unsuccessfully to get Galileo a professorship at the University of Padua. But, some time later, the position of Professor of Mathematics became vacant at the University of Pisa. Through his network of influential friends, the Marquis was able to persuade the authorities to hire Galileo.

In 1589, thanks to his rich friend's persistence, Galileo moved back to the university and began his new career.

The job paid very poorly and was considered the least significant post of all the professorships at the university. Galileo's salary at the time was less than one thirtieth of that paid to a highly respected Professor of Medicine at the same university! But, it was certainly an improvement on scraping together a living as a private tutor.

Pisa Again

Back at the University of Pisa, twenty-five-year-old Galileo continued pushing his anti-Aristotelian propositions. This time, it landed him in trouble.

It was one thing for a fresh-faced undergraduate to suggest radical ideas, but quite another for the Professor of Mathematics at one of Italy's most respected universities to be so controversial.

Galileo seems to have either been totally unaware of the antagonism his views produced or was deliberately trying to cause trouble. In his first year, he published a satirical pamphlet mocking the strict rules of the university and ridiculing what he saw as the pompous action of some of his colleagues.

Then he severely and publicly criticized a scheme to dredge a nearby port that would have made a great deal of money for a local property developer. This businessman, it turns out, was a good friend of the head of the university.

Some good things did, however, eventually come from Galileo's actions.

The continued refusal of his colleagues to let go of their Aristotelian attitudes encouraged Galileo to do some of his most important work in physics—and partly as an act of rebellion. In particular, he was angered by his associate's refusal to accept that Aristotle was wrong on the question of what happened to objects when allowed to fall from a resting position.

In 1590, he brought together all of his developing ideas on motion and falling bodies in a book called *De Motu*, "On Motion."

"De Motu"

De Motu cannot be called a great work of science. A number of ideas suggested by Galileo were not fully developed at the time of writing, and in places the text is a strange blend of science and

"I am sure that if Aristotle should return to Earth, he would rather accept me among his followers, in view of my few but conclusive contradictions, than a great many other people who, in order to sustain his every saying as true, go pilfering conceptions from his texts that never entered his head."

—Galileo

imagination. Galileo realized this soon after it was completed. He was particularly self-critical over the fact that, at times, he had been breaking his own "golden rule" and had not supported his ideas with real experimental evidence.

Just as the book was about to go to press, he withdrew the manuscript and it was only published in a far more developed form many years later.

Aristotle had stated that objects of different weight fell at different speeds. Galileo was convinced that this idea was completely wrong. Instead, he believed that all objects fell at the same speed regardless of their weight.

This was not an original idea; other scientists had suggested it before. In particular, a Flemish engineer Simon Stevin, a contemporary of Galileo's, had conducted experiments on falling lead weights, and written an account of his work.

Not long after Galileo withdrew his book, these arguments came to a head. He decided to produce a clear and convincing demonstration to show that the Greek philosopher had been wrong, and his old ideas needed reworking.

The Leaning Tower of Pisa

There were many famous incidents in Galileo's long life, remembered and recorded by later generations. Probably the most popular story is one involving an experiment he is said to have conducted from the top of the Leaning Tower of Pisa in 1591.

Pisa's extraordinary building was built in 1174 and, from the earliest times, began to lean. It is now some 17 feet (5 meters) out of perpendicular. By the sixteenth century, the Leaning Tower of Pisa had become a landmark and attracted the attention of visitors from all over Italy. It was here that Galileo decided he would provide a spectacular demonstration to prove Aristotle wrong.

This engraving was made from a classical bust of the Greek philosopher Aristotle. Aristotle was born nearly 400 years before Christ and, although he is recognized as one of the great thinkers of history, many of his theories were wrong. Despite this, the word of Aristotle was taken as absolute truth for nearly 2,000 years.

One of Aristotle's fundamental ideas in physics was that if two objects of different weight were allowed to fall under the influence of gravity, the heavier one would reach the ground first. But, as with all his propositions, Aristotle never tested the concepts with actual experiments. Despite the lack of observable evidence, Aristotle's theories were quickly accepted as fact.

To prove Aristotle wrong, Galileo climbed to the top of the Leaning Tower with two assistants and two cannonballs of different weights.

The climb was nerve-racking. To reach the top, he had to walk hundreds of worn and slippery steps, winding round in a steep spiral staircase inside the stone walls. By the time he reached the last step, he was sweating and weary. But, he had a job to do. Spurred on by his anger and frustration, he climbed on to the bell tower high above the upper platform of the tower. It leaned to one side at a frightening angle. He only just managed to ignore his feelings of dizziness and pressed on to the highest point.

He positioned himself at the edge of the bell tower with two cannonballs, 179 feet (54.5 meters) above the ground. At the base of the tower he could see his doubting colleagues from the university whom he had persuaded to attend. He stretched out his hand to test the breeze. It was calm.

The two assistants leaned over the edge. Each held a cannonball. At the appropriate moment, Galileo gave the signal. The assistants let go of the balls at the same instant, allowing them to fall under the force of gravity to the grass below.

It was clearly observed that both balls reached the ground at almost the same time. This proved beyond any doubt that two objects of different weights fall at the same rate of speed. Aristotle had been wrong.

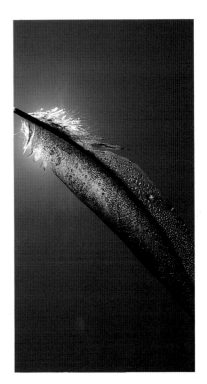

Opposite: *The Leaning Tower of Pisa*

Above: *If Galileo had used a lead weight and a feather in his famous experiment, the lead weight would have landed long before the feather because the feather experiences greater air resistance.*

Farewell to Pisa

The simple experiment at the tower showed that what Galileo Galilei and the others had said was true. The only force that could alter the speed of a fall was air resistance. Objects with large surface areas were slowed more than those with compact ones.

In fact, it would be fifty years later, soon after Galileo's death in 1642, that the Irish scientist Robert Boyle would conduct an experiment that confirmed Galileo's theory.

Boyle pumped all the air out of a glass jar and allowed a lead bullet and a feather to fall within the jar under the influence of sheer gravity. He found that the bullet and the feather reached the base of the jar simultaneously.

Galileo's success, however, was followed by disappointment. He began to hear reports that his contract at the university would not be renewed when the three-year term was completed.

Then, tragedy struck. In the winter of 1591, his father Vincenzio died unexpectedly, leaving the twenty-seven-year-old Galileo as the head of the family and responsible for their welfare.

Worse still was the fact that, before his death, Vincenzio had promised a large dowry to Galileo's sister Virginia.

During his life, Vincenzio Galilei consistently lost any money he had made by backing ambitious business projects that repeatedly failed. When he died, the Galileis were suddenly pushed to the edge of financial ruin. As the eldest son, the burden of sorting out the family's affairs fell on Galileo's shoulders.

More trouble lay ahead. Within weeks of his father's death, Galileo's contract at the university came up for renewal. He had created enemies with both his satirical literature and his ideas about the dredging of the local port. His anti-Aristotelian

Using the apparatus below in 1642, Robert Boyle found that if the air was completely removed from the glass jar, then objects as different as a feather and a lead bullet took the same time to fall the height of the jar.

opinions had turned his superiors against him. He held little hope that the university authorities would be sympathetic to his family's problems.

As he had feared, the request for renewal of his contract was turned down by the university and the professor was asked to seek alternative employment.

At that point, when all seemed lost, Galileo's friend, the Marquis del Monte, came to the rescue again. The wealthy patron helped Galileo secure a post as Professor of Mathematics at the far more liberal University of Padua.

By early 1592, Galileo had moved to Padua and taken up his new job at the university with a salary three times larger than he had received in his previous position.

Now he was able to support his mother, brothers, and sisters, and even started to pay off the promised dowry.

Padua

In the sixteenth century, Italy was divided into a number of independent states. Although each state had its own ruler, they were all joined in an alliance under the leadership of Rome. Padua, a city situated in the northeast section of the country, came under the sovereignty of Venice, 20 miles (32 kilometers) away on the coast. Venice was governed by a progressive noble family and was famous for its enlightened court. The University of Padua was a haven for radical thinkers like Galileo.

Academic groups had sprung up outside the university and among the intellectuals of the districts, where discussions of unconventional ideas were actively encouraged.

By this time, Galileo had made quite a name for himself as an anti-Aristotelian thinker and radical mathematician. He was welcomed with open arms by the intellectuals of Padua.

"Galileo Galilei not only relished his battles with the Church, but also enjoyed quarreling with the latter-day Aristotelians, heirs to the ancient science handed down through Islamic culture, to the Middle Ages. Galileo pictured himself as a heroic protagonist of 'The New Science' against the dogmatic absurdities of the 'Old Science.'"

—Colin Ronan, from "Man Masters Nature"

"Galileo thought that all he had to do was to show that Copernicus was right, and everybody would listen. That was his first mistake: the mistake of being naive about people's motives."

—J. Bronowski, from "The Ascent of Man"

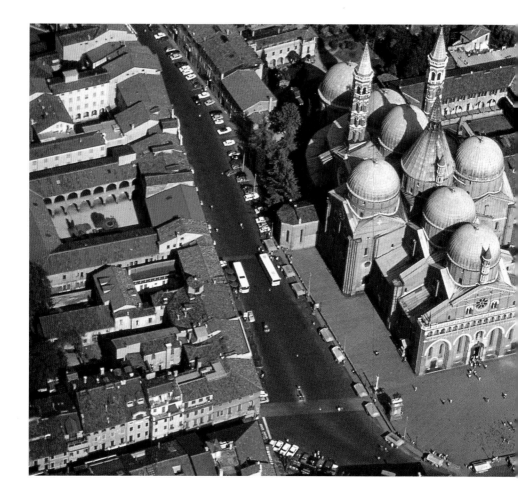

Galileo moved to the city of Padua in northeastern Italy in 1592. There, he took a position as professor of mathematics at the university.

As he grew older, Galileo lost none of his charm and easy-going nature. He made friends with a number of respected gentlemen and philosophers in the city quickly. He struck up a particularly close friendship with a rich nobleman named Gianvincenzo Pinelli. Pinelli was a man of great wealth with and insatiable desire for knowledge. He owned one of the most magnificent houses in Padua and a library containing over 80,000 volumes, making it one of the best in sixteenth-century Europe.

When Galileo first arrived in Padua, he lodged with his rich friend while the university arranged suitable accommodations for their new professor. The great advantage of this arrangement was that

Galileo had daily, uninterrupted use of Pinelli's extraordinary library.

Through his friendship with Pinelli, Galileo was invited to join the Pinelli Circle, which was sponsored by his nobleman friend and was the most influential of Paduan societies.

Galileo quickly became an important and respected member of the society. The members had regular meetings and weekly debates on scientific and philosophical matters. The Pinelli Circle became so prestigious that some members came from other states to attend meetings.

It was during his time at Pinelli's house that Galileo met men that were to later play very important roles in his life. He met them at his

"What made the Venetians hire him as their professor of mathematics at Padua was, I suspect, his talent for practical inventions. Some of them survive in the historic collection of the Academia Cimento in Florence, and are exquisitely conceived and executed. There is a convoluted glass apparatus for measuring the expansion of liquids rather like a thermometer; and a delicate hydrostatic balance to find the density of precious objects, on the principle of Archimedes. And there is something which Galileo, who has a knack for salesmanship, called a 'Military Compass,' though it is really a calculating instrument not unlike a modern slide-rule."

–J. Bronowski, from "The Ascent of Man"

companion's house on a number of occasions and became friendly with several of them. These men, who would eventually become leaders of the Inquisition, greatly admired Galileo's genius.

Happy Times

Life at the University of Padua suited Galileo, but despite earning a much larger salary, supporting his family proved difficult. Eventually, he had to tutor private students as he had done in Pisa.

He gradually built up a healthy tutoring business, teaching mechanics to military engineers, as well as giving astronomy and mathematics lessons to local enthusiasts.

Over the years things gradually improved and Galileo was able to buy a small house in the city. He began a relationship with a Venetian woman named Marina Gamba. The couple did not marry, but lived together for more than a decade, parting in 1610 when Galileo moved once again and left Marina in Padua. In the years they were together the couple had two daughters and a son.

Galileo showed little interest in marrying Marina and seemed during this time to have become increasingly preoccupied with his research. He never failed to provide for those who depended on him, but he could never be considered a loving parent or devoted partner.

This eighteen-year period in Padua was the happiest in Galileo's life, and it was also the time in which he made many important discoveries.

Problems to Solve

With the Leaning Tower experiment in Pisa, Galileo had shown that all objects fall equal distances in equal times, irrespective of their weight. But, he proved nothing about *how* they fell or whether they changed speed during their descent.

Once again, the fact that there were no accurate clocks available caused a problem. Unless it was allowed to fall from an extremely high altitude, it took a relatively short time for any object to reach the ground. The method of timing with one's pulse was practically useless for such experiments.

People are often surprised that Galileo did not return to his earlier idea for constructing an accurate pendulum clock. A possible reason for this is that it would have been too much of a distraction. Instead, he wanted to find a simple, quick way of measuring time periods that would solve the immediate problem.

Galileo made many of his greatest discoveries while at the University of Padua.

Rolling, Not Falling

Instead of releasing an object from a height and allowing it to fall freely, he thought of repeating the experiment by allowing balls to roll down a specially designed chute, inclined at an angle. This experiment slowed the descent considerably, without altering the basic motion of the ball. It was still falling under gravity, and if the effect of friction was ignored, the motion matched the movements of the cannonballs dropped from the Leaning Tower of Pisa.

The ball took far longer to reach the end of the chute than it did falling from a height. By lowering the chute to produce a small gradual decline, the ball could be made to move at a speed easily measured by another clever method.

Instead of measuring his pulse, Galileo set up a large barrel of water next to the experiment. At the base of the barrel there was a small hole that allowed the contents to empty gradually. The water was allowed to drip for the length of the experiment. He repeated the experiment many times and measured the quantity of the water collected in the bucket beneath the barrel.

Next, he altered the distance that the ball moved, and repeated the experiment using longer and longer journeys.

In time, a clear pattern began to emerge. This pattern led to the idea of acceleration.

The Idea of Acceleration

When objects travel at a constant speed, they cover equal distances in equal times. You experience this if you drive down the street in a car at a constant speed. It is only when objects speed up that they experience an acceleration.

It could have been that in Galileo's Leaning Tower experiment, the cannonballs were falling at a constant speed. But that would have meant they reached a steady and unchanging speed right after leaving the assistants' hands. This was obviously absurd. So, the only other possibility, it seemed to Galileo, was that falling objects gradually gained speed as they fell from a resting position. In other words, they accelerated.

To prove this, he set up the chute experiment and repeated the process of allowing a ball to roll different distances—timing the length of the journey.

In the first experiment, the ball was allowed to travel 8 feet (2.4 meters). This took two time units as measured by the dripping water. Next, the ball was allowed to roll 18 feet (5.5 meters). It was found to take three time units. Finally, the ball was allowed to travel 32 feet (9.75 meters) along the chute. This journey took four time units. At once, Galileo saw a pattern.

The difference in time units between the first and second experiment was 10 feet (3 meters) (18 minus 8), yet the ball covered the last 10 feet in the same time it took to travel 8 feet in the first experiment. In the third experiment, the ball went 14 feet (4.2 meters) further than in the second experiment (32 minus 18), and yet it did this in the same time as it took to travel 8 feet in the first experiment and 10 feet in the second—one time unit. So, it seemed obvious that the farther the ball went, the greater its final speed.

If this seems difficult to believe, think about what the average speed of each ball would be at the end of each experiment.

The average speed can easily be calculated by dividing the distance the ball rolled by the time it took for the journey.

In the first experiment, when the ball rolled a distance of 8 feet in two time units, the average speed at the end of the journey was 4 feet per time unit ($8 \div 2 = 4$). In the second experiment, the ball would have an average speed of $18 \div 3$, or 6 feet per time unit. In the third experiment, when the ball covered a distance of 32 feet, the speed would be 8 feet per time unit.

The only thing to affect the time taken for a ball's journey, either along the slope or falling vertically, was the distance it fell. If two objects, whatever their weight, were allowed to fall or roll equal distances along the chute, they would finish at the same time.

The Study of Ballistics

Galileo described the details of his findings in notebooks. He sent a long letter describing experiments to a good friend from the Pinelli Circle—the Venetian physicist Paolo Sarpi.

At this time, Galileo was earning extra income from designing and selling mechanical calculating devices to Venetian military leaders. It was through this contact that he became interested in the subject of ballistics, the study of projectiles.

Conventional physics stated that only one force could act on an object at any one instant, but Galileo was able to destroy this idea by performing a simple "thought experiment." This experiment is

This painting depicts Galileo (red robe, reading) demonstrating his acceleration experiment. The Leaning Tower can be seen in the background.

performed only in the scientist's mind—the process is described in detail, but the experiment is never actually performed.

Galileo pointed out that if a ball was dropped from the top of a ship's mast, the ball landed at the base of the mast and not halfway along the deck, yet the ship was moving. Obviously, the ball was experiencing the same motion as the ship. So, not only was the ball acted upon by the force of gravity as it fell from the top of the mast, but it was also experiencing the same forward motion as the ship.

It was clear that Galileo was right again. People has sailed the sea for thousands of years and no one had ever experienced an object landing a long way from the mast when dropped directly down.

Cannonballs

Galileo went on to use his findings to explain the motion of a projectile fired from a cannon.

He began by stating that the ball is acted upon by two forces—gravity and the initial impetus from the explosion inside the cannon.

Above and Opposite top:
*Two drawings·made
before Galileo's birth,
showing how Aristotle's
ideas were employed in
warfare. Aristotle thought
that a cannonball simply
flew in two straight lines
and dropped out of the
sky above the target.*

Opposite: *This illustration
shows the correct repre-
sentation of a cannon-
ball's path, which
appeared in Galileo's
"Discourses Upon Two
New Sciences."*

He showed that, if the force of gravity is ignored for a moment, then the explosion alone caused the cannonball to travel with a constant velocity. The fact that the cannonball was moving with a constant speed was obvious since the explosion inside the cannon only occurred once and produced no further boosts of energy. But from his free fall experiments, Galileo knew that cannonballs would also accelerate toward Earth due to gravity.

By careful experiments, he showed that the result of the two actions on the ball was to send it along an arched pathway called a parabola. The curve bent away from the originally straight course out of the mouth of the cannon toward Earth. By repeating his experiments hundreds of times, Galileo showed the greatest range could be obtained if the cannon was angled at 45 degrees to the horizontal.

Meanwhile, further blows to Aristotle's original description of the universe were about to be unleashed.

In 1597, German scientist Johannes Kepler published a book called *Mysterium Cosmographicum,* or "Cosmographic Mystery." This openly supported Copernicus's view of the universe. The book was based on the concept of a universe with the planets—including Earth—revolving around the Sun.

Kepler knew of Galileo's work and thought he may lend support to the anti-Aristotelian cause. He sent a copy of his manuscript to Galileo. The Italian scientist wrote to his German colleague praising his work and endorsing his revolutionary theories. But when Kepler wrote back and asked him to announce his support publicly, Galileo did not reply.

Although this may seem a rather hypocritical thing to do, Galileo was simply trying to avoid confrontation with Church officials. Kepler was living in Germany, a long way from the influence and power of the tyrannical Roman Catholic Church. In Padua, Galileo was on Rome's doorstep, in the very heartland of extremist ferment. At that time he was not prepared to announce his anti-Aristotelian views publicly.

Supernova

Seven years later, in 1604, a rare astronomical event occurred that again sent ripples through the scientific community. A supernova appeared in the night sky, outshining everything but the Moon.

A supernova is really an exploding star—they have only been recorded on a few occasions. No one in 1604 knew what had caused the supernova.

Aristotle had stated that the universe was constant and unchanging. But, if this was the case, what was the strange object that had suddenly appeared in the sky?

The Birth of the Telescope

In July 1609, when Galileo was forty-five years old, he went to visit his friend Paolo Sarpi in Venice. While he was there, Sarpi mentioned that he had heard through his foreign contacts that a Dutch spectacle-maker, Hans Lipperhey, had invented an instrument he called a telescope. Sarpi briefly described the device as being made by placing two lenses at the opposite ends of a tube. When directed at a distant object, a magnified image could be seen by placing one end of the tube to the eye and looking through the two lenses. Galileo was intrigued.

He rushed home to Padua and set about designing and constructing his own version.

This photograph of a supernova was taken in 1987. It was the brightest observed supernova since the one seen by Galileo nearly 400 years earlier.

The Dutch optician, Hans Lipperhey, is credited with inventing the earliest form of telescope.

A number of different telescope designs began to appear in scientific circles. Most were imported from other parts of Europe and were of very poor quality, giving a fuzzy image and low magnification.

Most people saw these telescopes as mere novelties and cared little for their quality. Galileo set his mind to radically improving these devices and producing a usable scientific instrument.

He ground his own lenses to a highly polished finish and masked off the front lens of the telescope so that light could not pass through its extreme edges and distort the image. By making these fairly simple modifications, he was able to greatly improve the magnifying power of the device to produce a far clearer image.

A Golden Opportunity

Galileo's improvements came just at the right time. In 1609, Sarpi heard that the ruler of the Venetian state, the Doge of Venice, had been offered a telescope at a very high price by a foreign designer.

The Doge had come to Sarpi for advice on the matter. When he discovered what a poor image the telescope produced and that it only magnified three times, Sarpi immediately advised against buying it. Instead, knowing his friend Galileo had improved the design of his own telescope, he persuaded the rich Venetian ruler to buy Galileo's instrument.

Galileo had indeed been making great advances. While most available telescopes were barely producing three times the magnification, Galileo had obtained magnifications of nine times.

Galileo's device was obviously of great use to the Doge. Venice was a maritime state that protected a small empire in the Adriatic Sea. A telescope of this type could have immense military use.

With Sarpi's influence, the Doge made Galileo an offer of a lifetime. He would take the telescope and, in exchange, give Galileo a permanent, life-long post at the University of Padua and a massive pay raise quite unheard of for a mathematician.

But Galileo was not totally convinced. On one hand he was very comfortable in Padua. He was happy with Marina, and the children enjoyed living in the city. But, he felt restless. He needed to work and live in a larger city. The University of Padua was well respected, but he needed greater support for his work at a bigger university. Communications were improving all the time and he wanted his work to reach a wider public. He wanted wider recognition and had grown tired of teaching at the university. He wanted more time for his research and resented wasting it on his teaching commitments.

However, the Doge's offer was exceptional, and there were no others to compete with it. After much deliberation, Galileo decided to accept the terms of the agreement and prepared the latest model of his telescope to hand over to its new owner.

Shifting Allegiances

Unfortunately, the contract of the agreement from the Doge of Venice was totally different from the verbal promises he had made. The pay raise was nothing like the one promised, and there were a number of unpleasant conditions written into the contract to which Galileo had no desire to agree. If he agreed to the terms, he would forfeit any future pay raises and would have to lecture on a regular basis until he retired.

Galileo immediately began to look elsewhere for a new position. He had heard that the position of court mathematician at Florence had become vacant. He made a hasty visit to show off his new telescope to the ruler of Florence, the Grand Duke Cosimo.

After a series of dramatic demonstrations that highlighted the telescope's power, Cosimo was

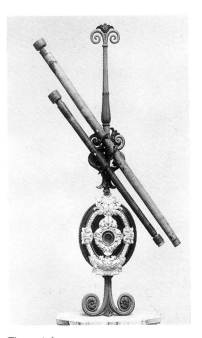

These telescopes were designed and built by Galileo. Both are now preserved in Florence. The earliest telescopes probably magnified more than a factor of two, but Galileo's telescopes were far more sophisticated. The larger of the two has a magnification of 14 and the smaller, a magnification of 20.

This painting shows Galileo presenting his telescope to the Doge of Venice.

convinced that this amazing device was the greatest invention of mortal man. And, its creator was offering his services at a very reasonable price. Within twenty-four hours of his arrival at the Florentine court, Cosimo had acquired the talents of the great inventor, Galileo. The scientist would move there as soon as possible.

Back in Padua, Galileo continued experimenting with his wonderful new device. The first thing he studied through his telescope was the Moon. And, in doing so, he ran once again into conflicts with Aristotle's theories.

Aristotle had stated that the Moon was a perfect and unblemished sphere, but even a casual observation with a telescope revealed craters covering the surface. On the first night of the observation it became abundantly clear that there were even more impressive objects on the Moon's surface. Everywhere Galileo looked, between the craters and crevices were towering mountains!

Galileo was able to calculate the height of these mountains by measuring the length of the shadows they cast on the surface. It was then that he received the greatest shock of all. He found that some of them were greater than the known mountains of Earth!

After studying the Moon, Galileo turned his telescope to the planets, and in early 1610, made one of his greatest discoveries.

Night after night, he observed black dots against the bright surface of the planet Jupiter. The strange thing was that these black dots were moving at a steady pace. Then one night, he turned his telescope toward the distant planet only to find that some of the black dots had disappeared.

At first he thought that the dots were a strange effect produced by some light reflecting inside the telescope barrel. But, by eliminating all possible problems with the telescope itself, he was forced to come to the only possible conclusion. Jupiter had moons that orbited the giant planet in the same way that our single Moon orbits Earth.

Venus

It was not until September 1610 that forty-six-year-old Galileo finally managed to arrange the move to Florence. Within a few days of settling in to his new home, he was working with his telescope again. It was then that he made another monumental discovery, but a discovery that would push him a step further toward trouble.

He began to make observations of the planet Venus. By observing the planet every night for several months, he realized Venus had phases—it went from looking full to barely being visible.

Photographs of the moons of Jupiter taken by the Voyager *spacecraft. Galileo could only see four moons with his telescope, but there are at least eight more moons.*

From Earth, the Moon appeared to shrink and grow during the month it takes for orbit. These are called phases of the Moon and people have been observing them since earliest times.

Like all planets and their satellites, the Moon does not produce light of its own. It can only reflect the light of the Sun. So, as the Moon passes between Earth and the Sun, we cannot see it because the light landing on the Sun side is facing away from us, back in the direction of the Sun. Gradually, as the Moon moves around Earth, more and more light is reflected our way, and we see more and more of the Moon until it reaches what we call full Moon. At this point, the Moon appears as a full bright circle, reflecting the light from the Sun directly to Earth.

If Venus also had phases, agreed the Aristotelians, then surely this was proof that it revolved around Earth just like the Moon. Once again, however, they were to be proven wrong.

This is the Villa Medici, the Florentine embassy in Rome. Well-connected in Italian society, Galileo stayed here whenever he visited Rome.

Galileo observed the planet for several months and found that the phases of Venus were much longer than those of the Moon. Whereas the Moon goes through all of its phases in one month, Venus takes nearly one-and-a-half years to complete its cycle! This, of course, would mean that the orbit of Venus around Earth would be far, far larger than was conceived by Aristotle.

A far simpler explanation was that Venus was nearer to the Sun than Earth, and that it orbited the Sun just like our planet. At one stage in its journey, it lies between Earth and the Sun and we cannot see it at all because we receive no reflected light from its surface. At the opposite end of the journey, it lies on the other side of the Sun from Earth and is fully lighted.

"The Starry Messenger"

In 1610, Galileo published a book called *The Starry Messenger*, in which he documented all his astronomical discoveries.

To flatter his new employer, the Grand Duke Cosimo II, he named Jupiter's moons after him in the text of his new work.

In March 1611, Galileo went to Rome and gave demonstrations of his new telescope and delivered lectures on his findings. This was partly to boost interest in his latest book, but also to serve as a means of building up a following in support of his anti-Aristotelian views.

Galileo was always an exceptional lecturer. Now, he captivated audiences with the amazing powers of his wonderful device. Once again, his charm and great powers of communication served him well. Before long, he and his telescope were the talk of Italy. Through the lens of the telescope, the audience could witness for themselves how the Moon looked huge. They could observe the Moon's craters and mountains and see how the planets looked so much

> "It is a most beautiful and delightful sight to behold the body of the Moon.... It certainly does not possess a smooth and polished surface, but one rough and uneven, and, just like the face of the earth itself, is everywhere full of vast protuberances, deep chasms, and sinuosities."
>
> —Galileo

> "I have seen stars in myriads, which have never been seen before, and which surpass the old, previously known, stars in number more that ten times. But that which will excite the greatest astonishment by far, and which indeed especially moved me to call the attention of all astronomers and philosophers is this, namely, that I have discovered four planets, neither known nor observed by any one of the astronomers before my time."
>
> —Galileo, from "The Starry Messenger"

larger than when seen with the naked eye. Astronomy was no longer a dull subject discussed by intellectuals and professors. Suddenly, anyone who attended the great scientist's demonstrations could experience its wonders for themselves. Still, support for Aristotle's ideas persisted.

When Galileo returned to Florence in June, he found that a group of philosophers and scientists, jealous of his public support and the admiring attitudes of the Grand Duke, had begun to plot and conspire against him. At every turn, they argued vehemently against his theories and attacked his work. The battle finally came to a head in 1612 with the publication of a book by a German Jesuit, Christopher Scheiner.

Scheiner had been using telescopes for a year or more. With their help he observed a number of dark marks on the surface of the Sun. He called these marks sunspots. However, Scheiner was a dedicated Aristotelian and believed that the Sun was unblemished. He proclaimed that the dark spots he had observed were tiny planets orbiting the Sun close to its surface.

When Galileo heard of this he immediately countered by taking his own observations and followed them with a treatise that totally demolished Scheiner's ideas.

A Burning Jealousy

A fiery dispute began between Galileo and the Jesuit. Scheiner was convinced that he was right, and drew on religion and philosophy for support. Galileo made his position clear and came down categorically opposed to Scheiner's. That put Galileo in a position that appeared to be heretical, turning against Aristotle and the Church.

Then in December 1614, the controversy expanded. A young priest, Thomas Caccini, began to preach

Opposite: *Galileo about age forty-six.*

Below: *Galileo first observed sunspots in 1611, which he sketched (top below).*

Bottom: *A recent observation of sunspots— these are about 3,500 miles across.*

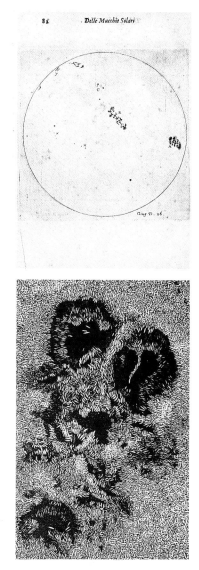

49

anti-scientific sermons from his church pulpit, specifically naming Galileo as an enemy of true faith. The fact that Caccini was questioning the scientist's faith came as a particularly painful blow to Galileo. He had always considered himself a devout Catholic and a true supporter of the faith. He never questioned God, only the narrow-minded attitudes of men. He did not see himself as a heretic, but as a thinker who wished to help others out of the darkness of blind faith.

In some ways, Galileo fell into a trap and lost his temper with the Aristotelians. He had always managed to avoid siding publicly with Copernicus. But, at the height of the controversy, he did just that. For once, his charm was not enough to help him. In a short book opposing Scheiner's supporters, he declared his convictions for Copernicus's theory that Earth was not fixed—it was simply a planet orbiting the Sun.

Within a few months, the dispute had come to the attention of the authorities in Rome. By spring of 1615, much to the delight of his enemies, Galileo had been summoned to Rome to denounce his support for Nicolaus Copernicus.

Galileo was perceived as being opposed to the Church and threatening the belief systems of future generations. The Church claimed that it was impossible for Galileo to be a scientist and a devout Catholic at the same time.

"The Assayer"

When he appeared before the pope's representative, Galileo withdrew his support for Copernicus and agreed not to teach theories that were sympathetic to these heretical views.

For a while things calmed down. But in 1618, three clearly observable comets appeared in the sky. A Jesuit scientist, Orazio Grassi, claimed that the comet's paths were straight lines and proposed

Opposite: *An Italian Catholic church of the early seventeenth century.*

Below: *A one-time mathematician and friend of Galileo, Maffeo Barberini. He became Pope Urban VIII in 1623.*

This illustration depicts prisoners undergoing a variety of horrible tortures at the hands of the Inquisition—all sanctioned by the pope.

a number of schemes to fit them into the old Aristotelian idea of Earth being the central point of the universe.

Breaking the earlier ruling from Rome, Galileo publicly denounced Grassi and the Jesuits by writing a book called *The Assayer.* It used Copernicus's theory to explain the observed path of the comets.

The comets' course could be followed by using a telescope. It was clear that their paths were not straight lines, but curved. By applying the most advanced mathematics of the day, Galileo was able to show that the facts alone fit perfectly into

"'Sympathy,' 'antipathy,' 'occult properties,' influences, and other terms are employed by philosophers as a cloak for the correct reply, which would be 'I do not know.' That reply is as much more tolerable than the others as candid honesty is more beautiful than deceitful duplicity."

–Galileo, from "The Dialogue"

Copernicus's scheme, and that once more Aristotle had been mistaken.

Unfortunately for Galileo, the authorities ignored the evidence and, once more, disagreed with him. As a result, in 1624, the sixty-year-old Galileo was summoned back to Rome.

Persecution

This time Pope Urban VIII—who had once been a friend of Galileo—was highly displeased and would not listen to Galileo's opinions. Fortunately, Galileo had built up lifelong protection for himself. Not only

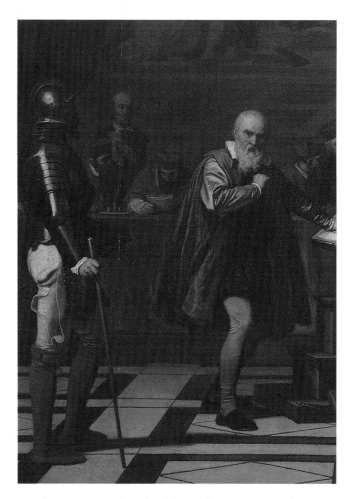

After refusing to write a book supporting views he knew to be false, Galileo was put on trial in April 1633.

was he a respected and celebrated scientist—perhaps the greatest in the day—he had also constructed a network of important friends.

His friends spoke out in support of him and managed to appease the angry pope by persuading Galileo to sign a decree that he would never again teach Copernican ideas. The pope accepted this. But then came a surprise.

The pope gave Galileo permission to write a book that would lay down the arguments from both sides of the debate. In the book he was to give a balanced account of the matter, but, in the end, must finally conclude that the heretical Copernicus was wrong.

If he was to return to Florence a free man, Galileo had no choice but to agree to the plan.

"Galileo, perhaps more than any other single person, was responsible for the birth of modern science. His renowned conflict with the Catholic Church was central to his philosophy, for Galileo was one of the first to argue that man could hope to understand how the world works, and, moreover, that we could do this by observing the real world."

–Nobel Prize Winner Stephen Hawking, from "A Brief History of Time"

House Arrest

Nine years after receiving instructions from Rome, Galileo finished his book, *Dialogue Concerning the Two Chief Systems of the World.* The book's final conclusion did not follow the instructions Galileo was given. Galileo was now summoned by the pope to stand trial for heresy.

Once again in Rome, the sixty-nine-year-old Galileo was treated like a criminal. His friends in the Inquisition undoubtedly worked hard to save his life and to persuade the furious pope to soften a probable death sentence to life imprisonment.

Galileo was placed under house arrest. He was allowed to live in a small house outside of Florence where he was guarded twenty-four hours a day

and was refused permission to travel outside of the grounds. All of his books were banned, their sale or distribution punishable by death. His letters to family and friends were censored, and visitors had to receive special permission from Rome before they were allowed to talk to the captive scientist.

Opposite: *Galileo ponders whether to publicly side with Copernicus, who is correct, or with the Church, which could spare his life.*

Surviving

At first, this terrible treatment took its toll on the great man. He fell into a dark depression that was further deepened by a series of physical and emotional blows.

In 1633, he fell seriously ill, struck down by a recurrence of an infection he had suffered before the trial. The authorities of Rome forbade him to travel to Florence for treatment and the illness grew worse. At the insistence of friends close to the pope, he was tended to by a visiting doctor.

Then, in 1634, his daughter, Marie Celeste, grew sick and died suddenly in a nearby convent where she lived as a nun.

Despite these hardships, Galileo was not beaten. He returned to his interests outside of science and began to paint, and play the lute as he had done as a child. After a while, he regained his burning interest in science and his greatest gifts of curiosity and imagination gradually returned. He began to write again, and in his final years he produced many influential discoveries in mechanics.

One of the few concessions the Church authorities made was that he was provided with scientific apparatus and he carried out nightly observations of the Moon, stars, and planets with his latest telescope.

"Two New Sciences"

Between 1634 and 1637, in those dark days of captivity, Galileo produced what many consider to be his greatest scientific work. He called the new book *Two New Sciences*. In it, using the familiar

• •

"At a very distant date in the future, the average mind may surpass that of Galileo to the same extent as Galileo's surpasses that of a child. And of all the infinite possibilities one may occur to a Galileo of the distant future, which when formulated as a law, may serve to describe motions of a body better than the laws he proposed in 1638."

—Albert Einstein

• •

technique of characters discussing the problems involved, he described two important, but very different areas of science.

In the first half of the book, he considered the subject of motion, how objects move, and the forces that operate them. In the second half, he dealt with the properties of matter, and how different materials can be stretched and shaped into various different forms.

This final text of *Two New Sciences* was truly revolutionary. The first half opened the way for the work of future generations of physicists. The most important of these was the great English mathematician and physicist Sir Isaac Newton, who was born the year Galileo died. It is a fascinating fact that Newton's work leads from Galileo's in an almost seamless path.

Secret Publication

The second half of *Two New Sciences* was totally new—no scientist had ever before considered the properties of materials in a mathematical way. The book suggests theories concerning a variety of things, from why it is that some materials are elastic and others are not, to why only certain substances conduct heat.

Galileo had not lost his touch—in fact, his genius had matured. The problem was, he was forbidden to have his work published. There was absolutely nothing heretical in the new book, but the declaration from Rome had been all-embracing. Galileo was to be totally silenced.

With the help of his friends, Galileo secretly contacted a printing company in Holland, a country far enough away from the influence of the Church to risk the pope's anger. The manuscript was smuggled out and, in 1638, Galileo's greatest work, *Two New Sciences,* was published.

Final Days

Galileo worked to the end. Science was in his blood. He lived for discovery, for the excitement of unveiling the secrets of the universe.

In 1637, within weeks of completing *Two New Sciences*, he was stricken with an eye infection, and soon his sight was completely gone.

He was allowed to employ assistants who carried out scientific observations for him, reporting

During his final years, Galileo suffered with blindness and relied on the observations of assistants to help him with his theories.

"Today news has come of the loss of Signor Galilei, which touches not just Florence but the whole world, and our whole century which from this divine man has received more splendor than from almost all the other ordinary philosophers. Now, envy ceasing, the sublimity of that intellect will begin to be known which will serve all posterity as guide in the search for truth."

–Cardinal Barberini

Viewed as one of the greatest scientists of history, Galileo's work laid the foundation for the development of many branches of science.

F Villamena Fecit

their findings for the great scientist to analyze and incorporate into his latest theories.

But, Galileo was growing weaker and becoming increasingly resentful of the conditions of his imprisonment within walled grounds.

On January 8, 1642, blind, scorned by his peers, and alone, Galileo Galilei died in his sleep.

Legacy from a Genius

What Galileo gave to the world of science is immeasurable. He laid the ground work for Newton's pioneering discoveries on force, gravity, and motion a generation later. And, in their turn, those principles of motion are still used to this day.

Galileo turned the telescope from a trinket into a scientific instrument of infinite use. He discovered the concept of acceleration, and put the idea into a mathematical formula that is used in almost the same way today. He revolutionized our understanding of what happens to objects in free fall and clarified this with simple, meticulous experiments never before imagined. By example, he opened up a whole new approach to science.

Galileo's greatest contribution, however, was to fight for the position of science in the world. He tried throughout his life to establish clear thinking in science and paved the way for revolution in human thought.

The antiquated religion that had punished Galileo and tried to break his spirit may have dominated his life, but it never managed to quell his genius.

The Roman Catholic Church ultimately failed to stop the enlightenment that science brought. Against the clear logic and uncompromising reason of Galileo, the false ideas that the Church cherished were finally swept away.

Thanks to Galileo, "The Age of Enlightenment" very soon began to grow at an unstoppable pace, spreading out across the entire civilized world.

Important Dates

1543	Nicolaus Copernicus's book, *The Revolution of Heavenly Spheres,* is published. In the book, Copernicus suggests that Aristotle's theory about the universe is wrong.
1564	**Feb 15:** Galileo Galilei is born in Pisa, Italy.
1581	**Sept:** Aged seventeen, Galileo becomes a student at Pisa University.
1583	Galileo begins experimenting with pendulums.
1585	Aged twenty-one, Galileo leaves Pisa University. He continues to study mathematics and begins to give private lessons.
1586	Galileo writes *Il bilancetta.* It brings him to the attention of other scientists and he begins to establish himself as a mathematician.
1589	Galileo, aged twenty-five, is appointed Professor of Mathematics at Pisa University.
1590	Galileo writes *De Motu* which brings together his ideas on motion and falling bodies.
1591	Galileo conducts his experiments from the Leaning Tower of Pisa. Galileo's father dies.
1592	Galileo's contract at Pisa University comes to an end and he is appointed Professor of Mathematics at the University of Padua. While in Padua, he has a relationship with Marina Gamba and three children are born.
1593	Galileo begins to investigate acceleration using an inclined plane.
1597	The German scientist, Johannes Kepler, publishes *Mysterium Cosmographicum,* which supports Copernicus's theory about the universe. **Oct:** A supernova appears in the sky, giving Galileo more evidence that Aristotle's theory about the universe is wrong.
1609	Galileo constructs an improved model of the telescope and begins his astronomical observations.
1610	**Mar:** Galileo publishes *Starry Messenger.* **Sept:** Galileo moves to Florence to take the position of mathematician to the Grand Duke.
1612	The German Jesuit astronomer, Christopher Scheiner, publishes a book on sunspots. Galileo totally disagrees with Scheiner's reasoning.
1613	Galileo's *History and Demonstrations Concerning Sunspots and Their Phenomena* is published. It shows that Galileo supports Copernicus's theory about the universe, not Aristotle's.
1614	**Dec:** A Dominican priest, Thomas Caccini, condemns Galileo for supporting Copernicus's theory.
1615	Galileo is summoned to Rome to denounce his support for Copernicus.
1618	Three comets appear in the sky, triggering further controversy between Galileo and supporters of Aristotle.

1623	Galileo publishes *The Assayer* in which he challenges the Church's thinking on the universe.
1624	Galileo is told by the pope to write a "balanced" account of the disagreements between the Church and Copernicus's theory about the universe.
1632	**Feb:** Galileo's *Dialogue Concerning the Two Chief Systems of the World* is published. **Aug:** The Church orders the sale of *The Dialogue* to be suspended. The inquisition summons Galileo to Rome.
1633	**April:** Galileo, age sixty-nine, stands trial. **June:** Galileo is found guilty. He is given a life sentence and placed under house arrest. *The Dialogue* and all his other works are banned.
1634	**April:** Galileo's daughter, Marie Celeste, dies. Galileo begins writing *Discourses and Mathematical Demonstrations Concerning Two New Sciences.*
1637	Galileo contracts an eye infection and loses his sight.
1638	*Two New Sciences* is published in Leiden, Holland.
1642	**Jan 8:** Galileo Galilei dies aged seventy-seven.

For More Information

Books

Dudley, Mark. *An Eye To the Sky* (Adventures in Space Series). Morristown, NJ: Crestwood House, 1992.

Fisher, Leonard Everett. *Galileo.* Old Tappan, NJ: Atheneum, 1992.

Graham, Ian. *Astronomy* (Science Spotlight). Chatham, NJ: Steck-Vaughn Library, 1995.

Hightower, Paul W. *Galileo: Astronomer and Physicist* (Great Minds of Science). Springfield, NJ: Enslow Publishers, 1997.

Ingpen, Robert. Jacqueline Dineen. Phillip Wilkinson. *Art and Technology Through the Ages* (Ideas That Change the World). New York, NY: Chelsea House, 1995.

Web Sites

Hubble Space Telescope's Greatest Hits
 Check out the gallery of amazing photographs featuring celestial objects seen through this extraordinary telescope—oposite.stsci.edu/pubinfo/BestofHST95.html.

NASA
 Learn about the latest space missions, earth and space science, launches, astronauts, and much more—www.nasa.gov.

Space Science Hotlist
 Explore links to over 200 great space-exploring sites including topics on planets, space research, galaxies, and astronomy—sln.fi.edu/tfi/hotlists/space.html.

Glossary

Acceleration: In physics, the rate of change of velocity with time. Generally, the ability to increase speed.

Area: In geometry, the size or extent of a surface measured in squares.

Atom: The smallest particle of a chemical element.

Ballistics: The scientific study of projectiles or missiles moving though the air.

Celestial body: Any object that occurs naturally in space.

Conduct: In physics, to transmit heat, light, electricity, or sound.

Force: An influence that is capable of changing a body's state of rest or uniform motion in a straight line. A force can act from the outside or the inside.

Formula: In mathematics and physics, a statement or law expressed using symbols. In chemistry, symbols that represent the composition of a substance.

Friction: A force that resists the movement of one surface against another with which it is in contact.

Geometry: The branch of mathematics concerned with the properties, measurements, and relationship of the lines, points, angles, surfaces, and solids.

Gravity: In physics, a force of attraction, acting between two bodies.

Mass: The amount of material in an object.

Mechanics: The branch of physics concerned with the study of moving objects and the forces acting upon them.

Parabola: In mathematics, a curve formed by a point that moves so that its distance from a fixed point is always the same as the distance from a fixed straight line.

Square root: In mathematics, a square root of a number is another number which, when multiplied by itself, produces the original number.

Sunspots: Dark patches that can be seen on the sun's surface. They are thought to be cooler areas.

Velocity: The speed at which an object travels in a particular direction.

Volume: In geometry, the space taken up by a three-dimensional object.

Index